With special thanks to -

James, for your endless advice and support, and
for eating the same recipes over and over;

Mum and Dad, to whom I owe a lot of things,
not least my love of food;

Jake, and my family at The Hug & Pint;

Vegan Apron (www.veganapron.com), with whom
many of these recipes started life;

And everyone who follows Morel Food.
I am constantly bowled over by your support
and enthusiasm.

Contents -

Foreword : New Traditions	7
A Word of Advice	8

The Recipes

i.

Lemon & Rosemary Roasted Almonds	15
Paprika Parsnip Crisps	16
Maple, Fig & Cashew Cheese Crostini	19
Ale-Battered Goujons with Dill Tartar Sauce	20
Walnut, Lentil & Fresh Herb Pâté	23
Leek & Potato Quiche	24
Wild Mushroom & Roasted Chestnut Soup	27

ii.

Seitan Wellington	33
Mustard & Maple Root Vegetables	35
Crispy Roast Potatoes	36
St. Clement's Brussels Sprouts	39
Redcurrant & Bramley Apple Sauce	40
Bread & Butter Sauce	43
Fresh Herb Stuffing	44
Red Wine Gravy	47

iii.

Madeira Plum Creme Brûlée	52
Dark Chocolate Mousse	55
Carrot & Almond Cake	57
Sticky Ginger Cake	58
Christmas Pudding with Brandy Sauce	61
Christmas Cake	63
Mince Pies	64
Cranberry & Pecan Cookies	67

iv.

Salted & Spiced Pecan Brittle	71
Whisky Tablet	73
Hazelnut & Amaretto Chocolate Truffles	74
Rose Turkish Delight	77

Foreword -

Traditions: we hold them in high regard. They're the backbone of all global societies; they're what we refer to when we want to know why or how to do something; they inform everything from our laws to the way we dress to what we eat, and often (or at least sometimes) with good reason.

What we tend to forget about traditions is their changeability. Though we may like to think otherwise, traditions aren't immovable or constant. On the contrary, they change endlessly. The traditions we keep now have altered in hundreds of ways over as many years and as many generations. And the traditions we pass on to our families and friends can be whatever we make them.

I thought my traditions were over when I went vegan. I thought Christmas as I knew it was over. I thought my favourite traditional foods- the meat- and dairy-heavy Lancashire fare I ate as a child, and the new foods I'd discovered when I moved to Scotland- were out-of-bounds. But I couldn't have been more wrong. I didn't need to give up my favourite foods; I just needed to rethink them. So I did, and I rethought my traditions too.

These recipes are some of the results of my rethinking. They're my old and not-so-old favourites, revised and reinvented for the people of a more ethical future. To me, they're meaningful not just because they're familiar and comforting, but also because they represent what vegan food can and should (I think) be: a melding of old and new, familiar and unfamiliar, traditional and radical. They demonstrate that going vegan doesn't mean giving up comfort food, memories, traditions, or Christmas- just animal products.

These recipes are my new traditions. They're better traditions. They're traditions I'll be proud to pass on. I hope they'll become your traditions too.

On practical matters -

Read each recipe thoroughly before you start making it (because there's nothing worse than getting halfway through and realising you're missing equipment or a key ingredient).

Understand that cooking times and temperatures are generally approximate guidelines. Everyone's oven is different; if yours normally runs hot or cool, adjust accordingly. Use your common sense and cook intuitively; you'll know (or learn) how to recognise when things are ready. Taste everything!

Most importantly - **have fun, and share at least a bit of what you make.**

On ingredients -

All of the recipes in this book are vegan: they contain no meat, fish, dairy, eggs, honey, or any other animal-derived products or by-products. When using foods which might not usually be vegan, for instance milk or butter, I try to specify "vegan butter", "soy milk", or similar. In any instance where I have omitted such specifications, assume I mean the vegan version of a food.

The following are ingredients which I use frequently and which are of special note.

Alcohol —
Check your alcohol is vegan before buying. Oftentimes alcoholic drinks (especially beers and wines) are fined using animal products; these can include isinglass (fish intestines), egg albumen, and milk proteins. Barnivore is a useful online resource for checking your alcohol; they also have an app called Vegaholic. Many supermarkets and smaller merchants now also label their vegan alcohol or have vegan lists available.

Aquafaba —
Aquafaba (AKA bean water!) is a culinary wonder. It acts as a binder and all-round texture-improver in baking, and it can be whipped up just like egg whites into meringues and mousses. For ease, I tend to use the aquafaba from tinned legumes (although you can make your own); pick beans packed in nothing but water, with no salt or preservatives. I have found organic chickpeas to be packed in the most consistently good (thick!) aquafaba, but butter beans, haricot beans, kidney beans, and black beans can all yield something similar.

Coconut oil —
While I don't think coconut oil is a miracle food (unlike a lot of people, it seems), I do think it's good for certain things. Its high percentage of saturated fat works in the cook's favour, because this allows it to set quite solid in the right temperature, which can help achieve certain textures. Always choose unflavoured coconut oil (unless of course you're making something coconutty), and check out Asian stores or the Asian section of your local supermarket, which will likely sell coconut oil for cheaper than health food shops.

Cream —
There are many good-quality vegan creams out there these days. I prefer unsweetened varieties which can be used in savoury recipes as well as desserts.

Flax seeds —
When combined with water, ground flax seeds (AKA linseeds) become a kind of all-purpose, edible glue that makes a great binder for vegan bakes. I buy my flax whole and grind it at home (mainly for reasons of cost), but you can also buy it already ground.

Food colouring —
A lot of food colourings, particularly red ones, are made from cochineal, AKA insects. Avoid any colourings with carmine, "natural red", or E120, which are all one and the same; ideally find one that's labelled vegan.

Kala namak (AKA black salt) —
Kala namak is a sulphurous seasoning known mostly for its eggy flavour. Use it sparingly in tofu quiches and scrambles.

Lemons and oranges —
Waxed lemons and oranges are often glazed with shellac (derived from insects), so always pick unwaxed citrus fruits.

Liquid smoke —
As its name suggests, liquid smoke imparts a smokey flavour to whatever needs it; used subtly, it can add a pleasant edge to certain savoury dishes. Always add liquid smoke gradually though, and taste as you do, because using too much can be ruinous.

Milk —
The world of vegan milks is vast and complex, and no doubt you will have your own go-to varieties and brands. I go for unsweetened soy, almond, and oat milks, though I mostly use the former in cooking and baking. If you prefer to use non-soy milks, feel free to do so.

Mixed peel —
Since it's made from citrus fruits, mixed peel can also be non-vegan due to the glazes used. Certain brands of mixed peel are labelled as vegan, so I tend to stick to those.

Mushrooms (dried, ground) —
Ground up, dried mushrooms are a great way of bringing some umami richness and "meatiness" to a dish. I tend to buy my dried mushrooms whole or chopped, then grind them up at home. Shiitake mushrooms are great for this purpose, but others work well too; I've had success with dried ceps or porcini mushrooms as well.

Nutritional yeast —
Like many vegans, I have a special place in my heart for nutritional yeast. Get the kind that's fortified with B12; it's an easy (and tasty!) way of getting your daily dose.

Seaweed (dried, ground) —
Seaweeds like kelp are excellent flavour-enhancers, and work especially well with mushroom and other earthy flavours; they can also impart a fishy flavour when needed. I use dried seaweeds, both ground and in the form of small pieces. For this reason, I generally just buy seaweed pieces and grind them myself as necessary. Kelp is probably my preferred seaweed, at least for these recipes, but other similar varieties may work too.

Sugar —
Sugar can be non-vegan as it's sometimes filtered through bone char, although it's mainly U.S. brands which do this. If you're not sure if your sugar is vegan, just have a quick look for it online.

The Recipes

i.

Lemon & Rosemary Roasted Almonds —

They're crunchy, they're lemony, and they're well, rosemary-y, and these almonds are the perfect pre-dinner or with-drinks nibble.

Serves: 4-6
Preparation time: 25 minutes

Ingredients -

250g almonds
1 tbsp extra-virgin olive oil
Zest of **1** unwaxed lemon
20g fresh rosemary leaves, finely chopped
A few big **pinches** of ground, smoked sea salt

Directions -

Preheat your oven to 175 degrees Celsius (350 Fahrenheit). Spread the almonds out on a large baking tray and dry-roast for 12 minutes.

Tip the roasted almonds into a mixing bowl and toss in the olive oil. Then add half the lemon zest, half the rosemary, and some salt (to taste), and toss again. Tip everything back onto the baking tray and roast for a further 4 minutes. Remove from the oven, return to the mixing bowl, and stir in the remaining lemon zest and rosemary.

Cool and serve. Store in an airtight container for up to 3 days.

Paprika Parsnip Crisps —

In general I'm not a fan of vegetable crisps, but for these and these alone I make an exception. In this recipe using parsnip brings a little something extra; the root's natural sweetness makes a great foil to the paprika and the garlic. I love paprika, so these are pretty heavy on the spice, but feel free to tone it down if you'd rather, or at least test as you add the seasoning.

Serves: 4-6
Preparation time: 30 minutes

Ingredients -

600g parsnips, washed and dried
1.5l peanut oil or vegetable oil
1 tbsp ground paprika
1/2 tbsp garlic powder
A **pinch** of chilli flakes
A **pinch** of ground black pepper
A **few pinches** of ground sea salt

Directions -

Using a mandoline (or a very sharp knife), slice the parsnips into even circles of about 1mm in thickness. Place these between a few paper towels and lightly pat away excess moisture.

Heat the peanut oil in a large, heavy bottomed pot (the oil should fill the pot to halfway at the very most). To be hot enough to fry, the oil needs to reach a temperature of about 190 degrees Celsius (or 375 Fahrenheit). If you have one, use a cooking thermometer to check the oil temperature, otherwise just drop a little piece of parsnip in- if it floats, sizzles, and quickly browns, the oil is hot enough to fry in.

When the oil is hot enough, gently add a handful of the sliced parsnips to the pot. Stirring gently, fry till crisp and golden-brown; they'll take 2 or 3 minutes tops. Remove the crisps with a slotted spoon or similar, hold over the pot for a few seconds to drain, then transfer to a wire cooling rack placed over a baking tray. Leave to drain while you cook the remaining parsnips, a handful at a time, repeating the process as before.

Once all the parsnips are fried, toss them in a large mixing bowl with the paprika, garlic powder, chilli flakes, black pepper, and salt (to taste).

Serve warm or once cooled. These crisps are best fresh, but you can store them in an airtight container for up to 2 days.

Maple, Fig & Cashew Cheese Crostini —

Hold a plate of these crostini at your next party and you'll be very popular. The secret to them is their moreish combination of flavours: sweet maple figs, herby cashew cheese, a hint of chilli heat, and smokey grilled bread.

Makes: 60 crostini
Preparation time: 8 hours 30 minutes (30 minutes active)

Ingredients -

For the cheese -
200g cashews, soaked in water overnight and drained
3 garlic cloves, peeled and roughly chopped
125ml soy milk
Juice of **1** unwaxed lemon
3 tbsp flavourless coconut oil, melted
1g fresh thyme leaves
5g fresh rosemary leaves, roughly chopped
(plus a little extra to top)
1.5 tbsp nutritional yeast
A **few grinds** of black pepper
A **few pinches** of smoked sea salt

For the figs -
8 large, ripe figs
2 tbsp maple syrup
1 tbsp extra-virgin olive oil
A big **squeeze** of lemon juice
4 or **5** dashes of Tabasco sauce (or to taste)
A few **grinds** of black pepper
A **pinch** of ground sea salt

For the bread -
1 or 2 good-quality baguettes (around **650g**),
cut into slices of roughy **1cm** in thickness
4 tbsp extra-virgin olive oil
1 whole garlic clove

Directions -

First prepare the cashew cheese. Add the soaked cashews, chopped garlic, soy milk, lemon juice, coconut oil, thyme, rosemary, and nutritional yeast to a food processor. Process till smooth or almost-smooth, depending on your preference, and season with salt and pepper (to taste) halfway through. Cover and refrigerate while you assemble the rest of the dish.

Next, the figs. Chop each fig into eighths and add to a mixing bowl. Toss well in the olive oil, maple syrup, lemon juice, Tabasco, and a little salt and pepper. Set aside to marinate.

Finally, the bread. Rub each one of the baguette slices with the whole garlic clove; drizzle with olive oil; then grill till crisp and nicely browned. The grilling is worth the effort for the smokiness, but if you don't have a grill pan, just toast them in an oven set to 170 degrees Celsius (338 Fahrenheit).

To serve, top each of the bread slices with a spoonful of the cashew cheese, a piece of marinated fig, a dribble of olive oil, a little rosemary, and an extra pinch of black pepper. These crostini are best eaten as soon as possible.

Ale-Battered Goujons with Dill & Tartar Sauce —

OK, so they're not necessarily a traditional Christmas dish, but my family always had goujons on The Big Day, and these deep-fried tofu goujons are so good I think they deserve a place at any festive feast.

Serves: 4-6
Preparation time: 1 hour 30 minutes (30 minutes active)

Ingredients -

For the goujons -
2 x 400g packets of extra-firm tofu
1 tbsp + 100g cornflour
125g plain flour
1 1/2 tsp baking powder
15g ground, dried kelp
165ml pale ale
165ml aquafaba
1l sunflower or vegetable oil
A **few pinches** of ground black pepper
A **few pinches** of ground sea salt

For the dill tartar sauce -
200g good-quality vegan mayonnaise
3 tbsp capers, roughly chopped
3 tbsp pickled baby gherkins, roughly chopped
5g fresh chives, finely chopped
5g fresh dill, finely chopped
A big **squeeze** of lemon juice
A **pinch** of ground sea salt

Directions -

Remove the tofu from its packaging, drain well, and press (either in a press or between some weighted plates) for at least an hour.

In the meantime make the dill tartar sauce. To do this simply combine the mayonnaise, capers, gherkins, chives, dill, lemon juice, and salt in a large mixing bowl. Decant the sauce into a jar and refrigerate till it's needed.

Once the tofu is pressed, cut it into sixteen even slices and season with salt and a little pepper on all sides.
Tip out the 100g of cornflour onto a large plate.

Place the oil over a medium-high heat in a large, heavy bottomed pot (the oil should fill the pot to halfway at the very most). Make the batter while the oil is heating. Sift the flour, baking powder, a tablespoon of cornflour, and half a teaspoon of salt into a large mixing bowl. Add in the kelp and combine well. Make a well in the centre, then pour in the ale and the aquafaba, stirring with a whisk as you do.

Check the oil is ready to fry by adding a little drop of batter; if it floats, sizzles, and browns quickly, the oil is hot enough. Take a piece of tofu and place onto the plate with the cornflour. Cover thoroughly in the cornflour, knock off any excess, then dip into the batter, making sure it's well coated. Drop the battered tofu carefully into the oil and fry till deep golden-brown. Remove with a slotted spoon, hold over the pan for a few seconds to drain, then place on a wire rack over a baking tray. Do the same with all the tofu pieces; you can normally cook three or four at a time.

Serve immediately with the dill tartar sauce and something fresh and green. The goujons should be eaten fresh, but the tartar sauce will store in a jar in the fridge for up to 5 days.

Walnut, Lentil & Fresh Herb Pâté —

I forgot how much I used to like pâté until I made this, which tastes almost (almost) meaty. But there's no liver here; the rich flavour comes entirely from mushrooms, walnuts, and fresh herbs.

Serves: 4
Preparation time: 25 minutes

Ingredients -

2 tbsp extra-virgin olive oil
5 garlic cloves, minced
1 small onion, roughly diced
250g chestnut mushrooms, roughly diced
250g black or brown lentils, cooked
100g walnuts
20g ground, dried mushroom
1 1/2 tbsp balsamic vinegar
1 tsp dark soy sauce
4 tsp nutritional yeast
2 tbsp flavourless coconut oil, melted
10g fresh rosemary leaves, roughly chopped
10g fresh sage leaves, roughly chopped
10g fresh chives, roughly chopped
1/2 tsp ground, dried kelp
1/4 tsp caster sugar
A good **few grinds** of black pepper
A **few pinches** of ground sea salt

Directions -

Heat the olive oil in a large frying pan over medium-high heat. Add the garlic and onion and fry till softened and starting to caramelise. Add in the mushrooms and continue to fry everything till nicely browned, stirring frequently. Then stir in the lentils, walnuts, and dried mushroom, and fry for another 5 minutes or so.

Add the mixture to a food processor along with the balsamic, nutritional yeast, soy sauce, coconut oil, herbs, kelp, sugar, and salt and pepper (to taste). Process on high speed until fully or semi-smooth, according to your preference (personally, I like a little texture in my pâté).

Cool, then refrigerate for at least an hour before eating. Serve with more fresh herbs, pickles, and toast, oatcakes, or warm crusty bread and butter. Store in an airtight container in the fridge for up to 4 days.

Leek & Potato Quiche —

Forget eggs, silken tofu gives you everything you need to make what a friend once called "the best quiche ever"!

Serves: 4-6
Preparation time: 2 hours 20 minutes
(30-40 minutes active)

Ingredients -

For the pastry -
250g plain flour
125g vegan butter, cubed and refrigerated
75ml cold water
A **pinch** of ground sea salt

For the filling -
2 tbsp vegan butter
1 onion, finely sliced
1 leek, finely sliced
2 small potatoes (about 200g), finely sliced
600g silken tofu, drained
1 tbsp gram flour
4 garlic cloves, roughly chopped
2 tbsp extra-virgin olive oil
150ml non-sweet soy milk
6 tbsp nutritional yeast
5g fresh thyme leaves
12g fresh chives, roughly chopped
7g fresh sage leaves, roughly chopped
3g fresh rosemary leaves, roughly chopped
Juice of **1/2** a small, unwaxed lemon
A **pinch** of kala namak
A **few grinds** of black pepper
A **few pinches** of ground sea salt

Directions -

Add the potatoes to a pot of salted boiling water and boil for 10 minutes, till slightly softened. Drain and set aside.

Melt the butter in a large frying pan over a medium heat. Add to this the onion and leek and fry, stirring occasionally, till golden and caramelised. Add the cooked potatoes and keep frying till everything is nicely browned. Take off the heat and set aside for later.

Add the flour and salt to a large mixing bowl and combine well. Add the cold, cubed butter and combine the two by rubbing gently through your fingers (alternatively, you can briefly pulse the flour and butter in a food processor). This should result in a sandy, breadcrumb-type mixture. You want this to be as even as possible (i.e. with no big lumps remaining), but don't overwork it. Start adding the water, a bit at a time, while bringing the pastry together with one hand. You may not need all of the water, or you may need a touch more; the pastry just needs enough to keep from crumbling, but not so much that it becomes sticky. Handle the pastry gently; it should come together with just a little light kneading. Once you have a smooth, coherent dough, wrap it in cling film and refrigerate for about an hour.

Preheat the oven to 180 degrees Celsius (356 Fahrenheit). Roll out the dough onto a lightly floured surface, making a circle large enough to cover an 8- or 9-inch quiche tin. Lightly grease the tin and place the pastry inside. Line the inside of the pastry with greaseproof paper and fill with pastry weights.
Blind bake for 10 minutes.

In the meantime make the quiche filling. Add the tofu, gram flour, garlic, olive oil, soy milk, nutritional yeast, herbs, lemon juice, and kala namak to a food processor. Process on high speed till smooth. Season with salt and pepper (to taste) and process again.

Remove the pastry case from the oven. Take out the pastry weights and lining and fill with the tofu mixture. Scatter the fried leek and potato mix over the top. Return to the oven to bake for 30 minutes, or till the top of the quiche is golden-brown and pretty firm when you shake it; a slight wobble is what you want. If the crust is getting too brown, cover it with tin foil.

Serve hot, or leave to cool completely then refrigerate for at least 2 hours before serving. Store covered for up to a day or two in the fridge.

Wild Mushroom & Roasted Chestnut Soup —

Great either as a starter or as a light bite, this umami-rich soup is intense, creamy, and satisfying.

Serves: 4-6
Preparation time: 40 minutes (15 minutes active)

Ingredients -

3 tbsp vegan butter
1 large onion, finely diced
5 garlic cloves, minced
2 celery ribs, finely diced
225g wild mushrooms (shiitake, oyster, chanterelles, or a mixture), finely diced
225g chestnut mushrooms, finely diced
20g ground, dried mushroom
100g chestnuts, roasted and peeled
1.5l good-quality vegetable stock
100ml non-sweet soy cream
2 tbsp nutritional yeast
1 tbsp fresh thyme leaves
A **squeeze** of lemon juice
A **few pinches** of ground sea salt
A **few grinds** of black pepper

Directions -

Melt the butter in a large pot over medium-high heat. Add the onion and garlic and fry till soft and beginning to brown. Add in the celery and all the fresh mushrooms and keep frying for a further 15 minutes.

Add in the dried mushroom, the chestnuts, and the vegetable stock. Bring to a boil, then reduce the heat and simmer for 45 minutes.

Remove from the heat and blend till smooth with a stick blender or a jug blender. Add the cream, nutritional yeast, thyme, lemon juice, plenty of black pepper, and salt to taste. Blend again, then return to the heat and simmer for a further 5 minutes. If you want a super-smooth soup, pass it through a fine sieve.

Serve with hot, crusty, buttered bread. To store, cool then refrigerate the soup; stored in an airtight container it will keep for up to a week.

28

ii.

Seitan Wellington —

A Wellington is a labour of love. You have to make the seitan, the pâté, and the duxelles, and allow for a lot of resting and cooling before you can finally assemble and cook the thing. But- and it's a big but- once the Wellington is assembled it really is a thing of beauty. If you want an impressive centrepiece for your festive meal, this is your guy. You can also make the seitan by itself if you want something a bit simpler.

Serves: 6-8
Preparation time: 10 hours 30 minutes (2 hours 30 minutes active)

Ingredients -

For the seitan -
240g vital wheat gluten
20g gram or chickpea flour
25g nutritional yeast
4 tsp garlic powder or dried, minced garlic
4 tsp onion powder
1/2 tbsp ground, dried mushroom
1/2 tsp ground, dried kelp
2 tbsp dried thyme
2 tbsp dried sage
A few pinches of ground sea salt
A few pinches of ground black pepper
2l good-quality vegetable stock

2 tbsp soy sauce
2 bay leaves
1 tsp liquid smoke
5 garlic cloves, crushed
5 dried shiitake mushrooms
6 black peppercorns
1 large red onion, finely diced
and fried until golden-brown

For the duxelles -
2 tbsp vegan butter
3 garlic cloves, minced
2 onions, finely diced

250g chestnut mushrooms, finely diced
5g fresh thyme leaves
5g fresh sage leaves, finely chopped
1 tsp ground, dried mushroom
1/2 tsp ground, dried kelp
1 tsp liquid smoke (or to taste)
1/2 tsp dark soy sauce
A splash of vegan sherry
A few pinches of ground sea salt

To wrap -
1 batch of walnut, lentil, and fresh
herb pâté *(p.23)*
1 x 500g packet of vegan puff pastry

Directions -

To make the seitan -

Add the dry ingredients (wheat gluten, gram flour, nutritional yeast, garlic powder, onion powder, mushroom powder, kelp powder, dried herbs, salt, and black pepper) to a large mixing bowl and combine thoroughly.

In a jug combine two cups of the stock with the soy sauce and half of the liquid smoke. Stir this mixture into the dry ingredients and a soft, pliable dough should form. Add the fried onion and knead the dough in the bowl just enough to bring it together, then shape into a loaf. Wrap the loaf tightly in tinfoil or greaseproof paper and bind with string; this will help it hold its shape during cooking.

Place the wrapped loaf into a large saucepan with the remaining broth, bay leaves, black peppercorns, liquid smoke, shiitake mushrooms, and garlic cloves. Cover and place over a low heat; simmer for two hours, or till the seitan feels firm when you press it. Flip the loaf over in the pan halfway through for more even cooking.

Remove from the heat and allow to cool in the broth. Store in the fridge in a sealed box with the broth overnight.

To make the duxelles -

Heat the butter in a large frying pan over medium-high heat. Add in the garlic, onions, and a little salt, and fry till softened and translucent. Add in the mushrooms and fry till everything is a nice golden-brown colour. Add the thyme, sage, dried mushroom, dried kelp, liquid smoke, soy sauce, and sherry, and keep frying till all the liquid is gone. Remove from the heat and leave to cool before using. You can make the duxelles while the seitan cooks and refrigerate them overnight too.

To make the Wellington -

Remove the puff pastry from the fridge about 30 minutes before you want to roll it. Preheat the oven to 200 degrees Celsius (390 Fahrenheit) with a large baking tray inside.

Remove the seitan from its broth (but don't throw the broth out) and place onto a few paper towels. Lightly dab with more paper towels to remove any excess moisture. Place in the oven on the baking tray to start heating while you roll out the pastry.

Roll out the pastry on some cling film into a large circle, large enough to wrap around the seitan with some overlap. Leave to rest for 10 minutes. Working carefully but relatively quickly, spread a layer of pâté onto the pastry, then a layer of the duxelles. Place the seitan in the middle and wrap with the pastry and the fillings; if you need, you can use the cling film to lift everything up and over.

Place the Wellington seam-side down onto the hot baking tray. Bake for 30-35 minutes, or till golden brown and hot in the centre.

Serve with traditional trimmings, or (even better) in leftover sandwiches! The Wellington is best fresh, but will keep for a few days in the fridge (although the pastry will lose its crispness); it can be frozen too.

Mustard & Maple Roast Root Vegetables —

Maple syrup and wholegrain mustard bring out the best in this classic combination of carrots and parsnips. Add a few herbs and you've got a side dish to be proud of.

Serves: 4
Preparation time: 45 minutes (5-10 minutes active)

Ingredients -

4 tbsp extra-virgin olive oil
1 tbsp apple cider vinegar
7 tsp wholegrain mustard
1 tbsp maple syrup
A **few grinds** of black pepper
A **few pinches** of ground sea salt
500g carrots, washed
500g parsnips, washed
5g fresh thyme leaves
5g fresh dill, roughly chopped

Directions -

Preheat your oven to 200 degrees Celsius (392 Fahrenheit). In a large mixing bowl combine the olive oil, vinegar, mustard, maple syrup, black pepper, and salt (to taste). Chop the carrots and parsnips into rough batons and toss in the dressing mixture.

Tip out onto a large baking tray, making sure you get all of the dressing on the tray. Roast for 30-40 minutes, or till browned and beautiful.

Once done, stir the fresh herbs through, check the seasoning is to your taste, then serve.

Crispy Roast Potatoes —

Everyone's got their favourite roast potatoes, and these are mine. Audibly crunchy on the outside, fluffy on the inside- what better way to mop up your gravy?

Serves: 4
Preparation time: 1 hour 15 minutes (30 minutes active)

Ingredients -

Enough sunflower oil to fill your roasting tin to a depth of 1/2 cm
1kg Maris Piper or Désirée potatoes
25g ground semolina
A **few pinches** of sea salt

Directions -

Switch on your oven at 225 degrees Celsius (437 Fahrenheit). Fill a roasting tin (pick a fairly thick-bottomed and heavy one) with the oil and place in the oven to heat up. Wait about 5 minutes before starting the next step; the oil has to be really hot when you put the potatoes in.

Peel the potatoes and chop into roughly even chunks. Place into a large cooking pot filled with cold water. Bring to the boil, add 2 or 3 big pinches of salt, and boil for 5-6 minutes. Drain thoroughly and tip back into the pot. Sprinkle the semolina over the potatoes then cover with a lid. Holding both the pan and the lid, shake up the potatoes in the pan. Give them a good bashing; this will help them crisp up in the oven.

Using a long-handled spoon or similar, carefully but quickly drop the potatoes into the sizzling oil. Give them a quick basting (carefully), then push them back into the oven. Roast for 45-50 minutes, turning the potatoes over halfway through.

Remove from the oven and, if you like, sprinkle with extra salt before serving.

St. Clement's Brussels Sprouts —

Forget the soggy sprouts of yore, these are roasted with orange and lemon for a zesty
citrus flavour and semi-crisp texture. Sprout-haters, consider this a challenge.

Serves: 4
Preparation time: 30-40 minutes (5-10 minutes active)

Ingredients -

600g brussels sprouts, ends and
outer leaves removed
3 garlic cloves, minced
Zest of **1** unwaxed lemon
Zest of **1** unwaxed orange
Juice of **1/2** an unwaxed lemon
3 tbsp extra-virgin olive oil
A **few pinches** of ground sea salt
A **few grinds** of black pepper

Directions -

Preheat the oven to 200 degrees Celsius (392 Fahrenheit).

Halve the sprouts and add to a large mixing bowl. Add in the garlic, lemon zest,
orange zest, lemon juice, olive oil, salt, and pepper. Toss the sprouts till well-coated
with the citrus mixture.

Tip the sprouts out onto a large baking tray along with all the citrus mixture. Roast
in the oven for 25-30 minutes, or till crisp on the outside and soft in the middle.
Give the tray a shake every now and then to help the sprouts brown evenly.

Check the seasoning, adding more salt or lemon to your taste, before serving hot.

Redcurrant & Bramley Apple Sauce —

On my table, this tangy sauce takes the place of more traditional cranberry condiments.
Smother it on your seitan, on sandwiches, and even on desserts; it's a good multi-tasker.

Serves: 12
Preparation time: 1 hour 35 minutes (35 minutes active)

Ingredients -

1 1/2 Bramley apples, peeled, cored, and
roughly chopped (about 450g)
300g redcurrants
250ml cold water
1/2 to **1 inch** of fresh ginger root,
grated (or to taste)
Zest and juice of **1/2** an unwaxed lemon
A good **squeeze** of orange juice
100g demerara sugar (or to taste)

Directions -

Add the chopped apples to a medium saucepan with
the redcurrants. Add the water, cover, and place over
medium-high heat. Bring to the boil and cook for
about 10 minutes, stirring occasionally as you do.

Uncover and stir in the grated ginger, lemon zest,
lemon juice, orange juice, and sugar. Cook down,
continuing to stir, for a further 15 minutes, or
till the sauce is reduced and thickened. Check the
sweetness is to your liking (I like mine quite tart),
adding more sugar if necessary. Remove from the
heat and, optionally, pass the sauce through a sieve
to remove seeds and pulp (I tend to just leave mine in).

Pour into a clean jar and leave to cool, then refrigerate
for at least an hour before serving. Store in the fridge
for up to 2 weeks, or for longer in the freezer.

Bread & Butter Sauce —

Buttery bread sauce: for when your Christmas dinner isn't quite as carbtastic as you'd like.

Serves: 6
Preparation time: 3 hours 30 minutes (30 minutes active)

Ingredients -

1 large onion
15 cloves
2 bay leaves
5 black peppercorns
550ml non-sweet soy milk
A **few pinches** of ground sea salt
120g white breadcrumbs
(readymade or from a stale loaf)
75g vegan butter
50ml non-sweet soy cream
A **few grates** of fresh nutmeg

Directions -

Peel the onion and cut it in half. Add to a medium saucepan with the bay leaves, cloves, peppercorns, and soy milk. Add a pinch or two of salt then place over a medium-high heat and bring to the boil. Remove from the heat, cover the pan, and set aside to infuse for about 3 hours.

Remove the onion, bay leaves, and peppercorns from the milk and place the pan over a low heat. Stir the breadcrumbs into the milk and add about half of the butter. Keep cooking and stir occasionally while the sauce heats and thickens. It should be ready in about 10 minutes, but you can make it as thick or thin as you like once the breadcrumbs have disintegrated.

Just before serving, stir in the rest of the butter, the cream, a little more salt (if needed), and the nutmeg; I like a good amount of the latter, but you can add as much as you like.

Pour into a hot jug and serve. This is best eaten on the day of making, but you can keep any leftovers in the fridge for a day or two (it will thicken up a lot though).

Fresh Herb Stuffing —
This flavourful stuffing is packed with fresh herbs, toasted nuts, and umami-rich mushrooms.
Eat it with your roast dinner or- even better in my opinion- on leftover sandwiches

Serves: 8-10
Preparation time: 1 hour 15 minutes (40 minutes active)

Ingredients -

60g walnuts, roughly chopped
60g pecans, roughly chopped
450g good-quality bread, roughly cubed
4 tbsp vegan butter
1 onion, finely diced
1 leek, finely diced
1 celery stalk, finely diced
4 garlic cloves, minced
250g chestnut mushrooms, finely diced
15g fresh sage leaves, finely chopped
15g fresh parsley, finely chopped
15g fresh thyme leaves
750ml good-quality vegetable stock
2 tbsp nutritional yeast
A **big squeeze** of lemon juice
1/2 tsp English mustard
1 tsp soy sauce
A **big pinch** of granulated sugar
A **few pinches** of ground sea salt
A **few grinds** of black pepper

Directions -

Preheat your oven to 175 degrees Celsius (347 Fahrenheit). Spread the walnuts and pecans out on a lined baking sheet and toast for 6-7 minutes, stirring them up every few minutes to allow for more even toasting. When the nuts are fragrant and just about browned, they're ready to come out. Remove from the oven and set aside on a cool plate. Leave the oven switched on.

Lightly toast the bread till browned.

Melt about half of the butter in a large, deep pot set over medium-high heat. Add in the onion, leek, celery, garlic, and a good pinch of salt, and fry till softened and translucent, stirring as you do.

Add the mushrooms and half of the fresh herbs into the pan with the onions. Keep cooking and stirring till the mushrooms have fried and browned and only a little liquid remains. Add in the toasted pecans and walnuts and stir well to combine. Cook for a further 2 minutes.

Add the stock and bring to the boil. Add in the remaining butter and herbs, the soy sauce, the nutritional yeast, the lemon juice, the sugar, the mustard, then finally the bread. Fold everything together till well-combined, and mash up any big bits of bread that are left over. Season with as much salt and pepper as you like and mix one final time.

Grease a large baking dish and pour the stuffing mixture in. Cover with tinfoil and bake for about 30 minutes. Remove the foil then bake for another 10 minutes, or till the top has crisped up and browned. Serve hot. Leftover stuffing will keep in the fridge, but might dry out, so it should really be made on the day of serving.

Red Wine Gravy —

Rich and flavoursome, this vegan gravy can stand up to any of its meaty counterparts.

Serves: 4-6
Preparation time: 2 hours 30 minutes

Ingredients -

6 tbsp vegan butter
5 garlic cloves, roughly chopped
1 large brown or white onion, finely sliced
2 carrots, finely sliced
2 celery ribs, finely sliced
Half a celeriac root, roughly diced
500ml good-quality vegetable stock
500ml red wine
4 sprigs of fresh thyme
1 sprig of fresh rosemary
5 dried shiitake mushrooms
1/4 tsp dark brown sugar
1 tbsp soy sauce
1 tbsp tomato passata
1 tbsp nutritional yeast
5 or **6** black peppercorns
A **few pinches** of ground sea salt
3 tbsp plain flour

Directions -

Melt 2 tablespoons of the butter in a large saucepan over medium-high heat. Add in the garlic and onion along with a couple of pinches of salt and fry for 5 minutes. Then add in the carrots, celery, and celeriac, and continue to fry until everything is golden-brown and beginning to caramelise.

Add the wine to the pan, keeping it over a medium-high heat for another 5 minutes. Add the stock, sugar, peppercorns, tomato passata, and the shiitake mushrooms and bring to the boil. Reduce the heat, add the fresh herbs, and simmer for about 2 hours, or until you have 500ml of liquid remaining. Strain and return to a low heat.

In a separate large pan, melt 3 tablespoons of butter over medium-high heat. Add in the flour and stir quickly to create a smooth roux. Bit by bit, add in the hot reduction liquid, whisking continually as you do to prevent any lumps from forming. Bring the mixture to the boil and add in the nutritional yeast and salt to taste. Reduce the heat to a simmer, continuing to whisk, for another 8-10 minutes or until the gravy has thickened. Whisk in the remaining tablespoon of butter to add extra gloss.

Serve immediately.

iii.

Madeira Plum Crème Brûlée —

Is that the sound of angels singing or the top of a crème brûlée cracking?
Because I can't tell the difference.

Serves: 4
Preparation time: 8 hours 30 minutes
(30 minutes active)

Ingredients -

2 ripe plums
A **generous splash** of madeira wine
3 tbsp demerara sugar
A **pinch** of ground cinnamon
A **pinch** of ground ginger
1 vanilla pod, innards of
3 tbsp tapioca starch
250ml non-sweet soy milk
250ml non-sweet soy cream
70g caster sugar
4 tbsp caster sugar (to top)

Directions -

De-stone and halve the plums and add to a small saucepan. Add in the madeira, the demerara sugar, the spices, and just a pinch of the vanilla seeds. Cover and place over a medium heat till the plums are well-softened. Once they're done, place them into the bottom of four ramekins or serving dishes (one plum half in each).

In a mixing bowl, whisk the tapioca starch into around 100ml of the soy milk. Combine the remaining milk, the remaining vanilla, the cream, and the 70g of caster sugar in a medium saucepan. Place over medium-high heat till almost boiling, then pour gradually into the tapioca mixture, whisking as you do.

When fully incorporated, tip the mixture back into the pan, continuing to whisk. Turn the heat up high and whisk quite vigorously till the mixture thickens. Carefully pour into the serving dishes on top of the plums.

Leave to cool, then refrigerate overnight (or up to 48 hours).

Remove the brûlées from the fridge and sprinkle each one with a thin layer of caster sugar. Caramelise the tops with a chef's blowtorch so they're an inviting golden-brown colour. (In a pinch you can also use a grill for this, but it's much more difficult to achieve an even result, and you risk heating the crème as you try to).

Serve with a little madeira on the side, if you fancy it. The brûlées are best eaten on the day they're made.

Dark Chocolate Mousse —

This mousse is intensely chocolatey, so you only need a bit to feel satisfied-although I wouldn't blame you if you ate the lot!

Serves: 4
Preparation time: 8 hours 30 minutes (30 minutes active)

Ingredients -

100g good-quality vegan dark chocolate, chopped into small, even pieces
A **pinch** of ground sea salt
1 tbsp icing sugar
Aquafaba from **1 x 400g** tin of organic chickpeas in water (no salt or preservatives) (about 120ml)

Directions -

Melt the chocolate in a bain-marie (or a heatproof bowl set over a saucepan of simmering water), stirring to help distribute the heat. Mix in the salt, then remove from the heat and set aside to cool slightly.

Add the aquafaba to a very clean mixing bowl. Beat with an electric whisk until fluffy and pretty stiff, adding the icing sugar in halfway through. This should take about 5 minutes in total.

With a spatula, carefully fold the melted chocolate into the foam, one spoonful at time. Be very gentle; the more air you can keep in the mixture the better.

Pour the mousse into serving dishes of your choosing and leave covered in the refrigerator overnight; they'll keep there for a maximum of 2 days.

Serve by itself or with your favourite accompaniments.

Carrot & Almond Cake —

This smarter-than-your-average carrot cake is made not with flour but with ground almonds, which give it a lovely texture. With a dollop of whipped cream or ice cream, this everyday cake becomes something very special.

Makes: one 8 inch cake
Preparation time: 55 minutes
(10 minutes active)

Ingredients -

2 tbsp ground flax seeds
Aquafaba from **1 x 400g** tin
of organic chickpeas (120ml)
160g vegan butter, melted
(plus extra to grease the tin)
160g caster sugar
1/2 tsp vanilla extract
1 tsp almond extract
250g ground almonds
1/4 tsp ground nutmeg
1/2 tsp ground cinnamon
1/2 tsp ground ginger
3 carrots, washed and grated
(about 225g)
80g currants
Zest and juice of **1** small,
unwaxed lemon
Zest and juice of **1/2** an
unwaxed orange
30g flaked almonds
30g golden caster sugar

Directions -

Preheat the oven to 175 degrees Celsius (347 Fahrenheit). Grease an 8-inch cake tin with vegan butter and line with greaseproof paper.

Combine the ground flax and the aquafaba in a small bowl and set aside. Add the butter and sugar to a large mixing bowl and whip together with an electric whisk (or a hand whisk and some elbow grease). Continue whisking, adding in the vanilla extract and almond extract as you do, then the flax mixture. When that's incorporated, use a spatula to fold in the ground almonds, spices, carrots, currants, lemon zest, lemon juice, and orange zest and juice. Combine well, but don't over-mix.

Scrape the batter out into the lined cake tin and sprinkle the flaked almonds then the golden caster sugar over the top of the cake.

Bake the cake in the oven for 45-50 minutes, or until golden-brown and slightly risen. It won't rise a huge amount, but a skewer stuck in the middle will come out clean when it's ready.

Let the cake cool in its tin before slicing and serving with your favourite vegan cream or ice cream (you can eat it warm too, but it'll be a bit crumblier). Store in an airtight container for up to a week.

Sticky Ginger Cake —

This recipe is based on the Parkin recipe my mum used to make around Bonfire Night, as is traditional in Lancashire. It's got a wonderful texture, and gets moister and stickier the longer you leave it. If you can, try and wait for at least a day before digging in- although this will be hard as it'll smell so good!

Makes: one 6 or 7 inch loaf
Preparation time: 1 hour 20 minutes

Ingredients -

100g vegan butter, plus extra for greasing
75g dark muscovado sugar
150ml golden syrup
150ml black treacle
5 tsp ground ginger
2 tsp mixed spice
1 tsp baking soda
2.5 tsp baking powder
2 tsp apple cider vinegar
275g flour
A **pinch** of ground sea salt
300ml non-sweet soy milk

Directions -

Grease and line a loaf tin and preheat the oven to 175 degrees Celsius (347 Fahrenheit).

Add the vegan butter, sugar, syrup, and treacle to a small saucepan. Heat gently over a low to medium heat until the butter has melted. Take off the heat and stir in the spices; mix well.

Sift the flour, baking soda, and baking powder into a large mixing bowl, and make a well in the centre with a spoon.

Add the soy milk and vinegar to a jug, mix well, and set aside.

Tip the warm butter/sugar mixture into the flour mixture, stirring constantly as you do, till fully incorporated. Do the same with the milk mixture. Mix till smooth, but don't overwork it.

Pour the finished batter into the tin and bake for 30 minutes, or till browned, risen and a skewer inserted in the centre comes out clean. Resist the temptation to open the door for as long as possible- the cake may lose its rise if you do!

Remove the cake from the oven, tap the tin sharply on a work surface or table, then leave to cool and mature. Serve by itself, or with some good-quality vanilla ice cream.

Christmas Pudding with Brandy Sauce —
The richest and booziest of all puddings, this is just the thing to prepare you for a lie down and a snooze. Fry up any leftovers and serve them with vegan cream for a ridiculously decadent Boxing Day brunch.

Makes: one very large pudding (2.4l) or several smaller ones
Preparation time: 16 hours 30 minutes (30 minutes active)

Ingredients -

For the pudding -

260g vegetable suet
110g self-raising flour
225g white breadcrumbs
(readymade or from a stale loaf)
1 1/2 tsp ground mixed spice
1/2 tsp ground nutmeg
1 tsp ground cinnamon
2 tsp ground ginger
450g soft brown sugar
225g sultanas
225g raisins
575g currants

90g mixed peel
30g blanched almonds, chopped small
30g pecans, chopped small
1 Bramley apple, grated (about 300g)
Zest of 2 unwaxed oranges
Zest of 1 unwaxed lemon
4 tbsp ground flax seeds
Aquafaba from 2 x 400g tins of
organic chickpeas (about 240ml)
100ml vegan whisky
300ml vegan stout
Vegan butter (to grease the basin)

For the brandy sauce -

60g vegan butter
60g plain flour
600ml non-sweet soy milk, hot
60g caster sugar
6 tbsp vegan brandy
A few grates of fresh nutmeg

Directions -

Put the suet, flour, breadcrumbs, spices, and sugar into a very large mixing bowl, and combine thoroughly. Then, one at a time, add in the dried fruit, mixed peel, almonds, pecans, apple, and orange and lemon zest, making sure that each ingredient is fully incorporated before adding the next.

Place the flax seeds in a separate mixing bowl. Mix in the aquafaba and beat for about 2 minutes with an electric whisk. Add in the whisky and stout and beat for a further 30 seconds. Pour this mixture over the dry ingredients and stir the whole thing till well-combined; this will take some elbow grease! Cover the bowl with a cloth and set aside overnight.

The next day, grease your pudding basin (or basins) with a little vegan butter. Spoon the mixture into the basin, packing it down with your spoon as you do; you want the mixture to be quite tightly packed. When the basin is full, cut out a square of greaseproof paper that's 3-4 centimetres bigger than the top of the basin; tie this tightly on top with some string, along with a plain cotton cloth of the same size (or one that's folded to be the same size).

Place a small saucer or similar upside-down in a large, lidded cooking pot. Put the pudding (cloth-upwards) on top of the plate.

Fill the pan with water so it reaches about a third to a half of the way up the pudding basin. Place over a high heat till the water boils, then reduce to a low simmer and cover the pot. Steam in this way for 6 hours, topping up the water periodically (adjust the time accordingly if you're making smaller puddings).

Once the pudding is cooked, replace the greaseproof paper (again tying tightly), and keep it in its basin in a cool place till you need it; its flavour will improve with several weeks of resting.

Reheat the pudding by steaming again for 2 hours, and make the brandy sauce about 20 minutes before you want to serve it. To do this, melt the butter in a medium saucepan over medium heat. Stir in the flour so a paste forms and cook this for a minute or so. Then, gradually pour the hot milk into the mixture, beating with a hand whisk to break up any lumps. Reduce the heat and simmer for 5-10 minutes; when the mixture thickens up, mix through the brandy, sugar, and nutmeg (to taste). Pour into a hot serving jug and enjoy!

Christmas Cake —

Christmas without a Christmas cake? That sounds like risky business to me.
You'd better make this, just to be safe.

Makes: one 8 inch cake
Preparation time: 12 hours 30 minutes (30 minutes active)

Ingredients -

175g sultanas
175g raisins
275g currants
100g glacé cherries, chopped small
100g organic dried apricots, chopped small
90g mixed peel
250ml good-quality vegan brandy
3 tbsp ground flax seeds
225g plain flour
1/4 tsp ground nutmeg
1/2 tsp ground ginger
3/4 tsp ground mixed spice
225g vegan butter, melted
(plus extra to grease the tin)
235g dark muscovado sugar
1 tbsp black treacle
1 tsp vanilla extract
Zest of **1 1/2** unwaxed lemons
Zest of **1 1/2** unwaxed oranges
70g blanched almonds, chopped small
Plenty of brandy (for feeding)
500g ready-to-roll marzipan
500g ready-to-roll white icing

Directions -

Place the sultanas, raisins, currants, cherries, apricots, and mixed peel in a large bowl and cover with 100ml of the brandy. Leave this mixture to soak in a cool place overnight.

The next day, preheat the oven to 140 degrees Celsius (284 Fahrenheit). Grease and line an 8-inch round cake tin with a double layer of greaseproof paper. In a small bowl mix the ground flax seeds with about 100ml of cold water. Place the flour, spices, vegan butter, sugar, treacle, vanilla, and lemon and orange zest into a large mixing bowl. Beat with an electric whisk till thoroughly mixed. Then add in the flax mixture (it should have turned gluey) and beat again. Fold in the almonds and the brandied fruits, together with another 150ml of brandy, and combine well. Spoon into the prepared tin and cover loosely with a round of greaseproof paper. Bake in the oven for about 3 hours, or till the cake is firm throughout (but still moist).

Let the cake cool in the tin, and if possible store it there too, covered up with cling film; otherwise keep it wrapped in the paper in an airtight container. Store in a cool, dry place for up to 10 weeks. Before storing, prick the top of the cake with a skewer a few times and drizzle over a few spoonfuls of brandy; feed the cake in the same way for every week or so of storage.

About a week before you want to serve it, cover the cake with rolled-out marzipan and icing, and add decorations as you wish. Store in an airtight container for up to 2 months.

Mince Pies —

These pies have a sweet, crumbly pastry and a richly spiced mince(non-)meat inside.
I like them best served hot with mulled wine or a good cup of tea.

Makes: 20 pies
Preparation time: 13 hours (45 minutes active)

Ingredients -

For the filling -

110g vegetable suet
175g raisins
110g sultanas
110g currants
100g mixed peel
175g soft dark brown sugar
25g almonds, chopped small
25g walnuts or pecans, chopped
small
1 small Bramley apple, grated
(about 250g)
2 1/2 tsp ground mixed spice
1/2 tsp ground cinnamon
1/4 tsp grated nutmeg
1 tsp ground ginger
Zest of **1 1/2** unwaxed oranges
Zest of **1 1/2** unwaxed lemons
A **pinch** of ground sea salt
140ml vegan brandy

For the pastry -

750g plain flour
A **pinch** of ground sea salt
475g vegan butter, cubed
and refrigerated
240g caster sugar
250ml non-sweet soy milk
(you won't need all of this)

Directions -

First make the mincemeat; start a day or two before you want to make the pies. Add all the filling ingredients and half of the brandy to a large, heatproof mixing bowl, and mix together thoroughly. Cover the bowl with tin foil and leave in a cool place overnight.

The next day, turn on the oven to 110 degrees Celsius (230 Fahrenheit). Place the covered bowl into the oven. Leave it there for 3 hours, or at least till the suet is fully melted. Remove and let cool, stirring every now and then as it does; this will allow the suet to set around the fruit. When the mincemeat is cool, stir in the remaining brandy, then set aside while you make the pastry.

For the pastry, combine the flour and salt in a mixing bowl. Add in the vegan butter, and rub between your fingertips to form a breadcrumb-like mixture. Rub in the sugar in the same way. Then pour in a little soy milk, a splash at a time, bringing the pastry together with your hands as you do; you won't need all 250ml of the milk, just enough to get a smooth, coherent dough. When the pastry forms a cohesive dough, roll it into a ball, wrap it in cling film, and refrigerate for 20 minutes.

Preheat the oven to 200 degrees Celsius (392 Fahrenheit). Remove the dough from the fridge and roll it out into an even circle of about two millimetres thick. Using a round pastry cutter, make twenty circles of pastry to fit twenty muffin tins. Press these into the tins, fill with mincemeat, then cut another twenty circles for tops (you may need to ball up and reroll the dough to do this, but if you do be as gentle with it as possible). Dab the bottom edges of the lids with a little cold water, then gently press them onto the top of the pies.

Using a knife, poke a couple of slits into the top of each lid. Bake the pies in the oven till crisp and golden brown (15-20 minutes), then dust with icing sugar and serve. Store in an airtight container for up to 3 days, or freeze for a few months.

Cranberry & Pecan Cookies —

If you can bring yourself to give them away, a batch of these lightly spiced cookies makes a nice little gift. Alternatively, you can eat them all yourself!

Makes: 15 cookies
Preparation time: 35 minutes (10 minutes active)

Ingredients -

2 tbsp ground flax seeds
150g plain flour
1/2 tsp baking powder
A **pinch** of ground sea salt
1/4 tsp ground ginger
1/4 tsp ground cinnamon
90g rolled oats
135g vegan butter
(plus extra to grease the tin)
100g soft dark brown sugar
75g caster sugar
25g golden syrup
1 tsp vanilla extract
100g dried cranberries
75g pecans, roughly chopped

Directions -

Preheat the oven to 170 degrees Celsius (338 Fahrenheit). Place the ground flax seeds into a small dish or cup with just enough water to cover them (about 30ml).

Put the flour, baking powder, salt, spices, and oats into a medium mixing bowl and stir briefly to combine. Put the butter, sugars, and syrup into a separate, large mixing bowl and beat until creamy with an electric whisk (or a hand whisk and some elbow grease). Continuing to beat, add in the vanilla extract and the flax mixture (which should now be a little gloopy), then the bowl of dry ingredients. When well-combined, fold in the cranberries and pecans with a spoon or spatula. Put the dough in the fridge for 10 minutes.

In the meantime, lightly grease one or two large baking sheets. When the dough is ready, take out about a tablespoon of it and roll into a ball. Place this onto the baking sheet and squish it down a bit with your hands or a fork. Repeat until all the dough is on the sheet. Bake for 15 minutes or till golden brown. Leave to cool on the tray for about 5 minutes, then transfer to a wire rack to cool completely. Enjoy with a cup of tea or a cold glass of soy milk. Store in an airtight container for up to a week.

iv.

Salted and Spiced Pecan Brittle —

Warn your teeth, because this stuff is addictive. Enjoy by itself (preferably snaffled out of a coat pocket on a cold day's walk), or on top of desserts.

Makes: a small tray's worth (roughly 25 pieces)
Preparation time: 1 hour (30 minutes active)

Ingredients -

150g pecans, roughly crushed
1/2 tsp ground ginger
1/2 tsp ground cinnamon
A big **pinch** of ground sea salt
200ml cold water
300g caster sugar
A few **pinches** of flaked sea salt (to taste)

Directions -

Line a small baking tray (mine is about 8 x 8 inches) with greaseproof paper. Add the pecans, spices, and a big pinch of ground sea salt to a small mixing bowl, and toss to combine.

Combine the water and sugar in a medium, heavy saucepan and place over medium-high heat. Bring the mixture to a boil, stirring occasionally as you do. Once it's boiling, reduce the heat to medium and keep cooking until the sugar turns a glossy brown colour (think conkers). When that happens (be prepared: it will take a while), quickly stir in the pecans, making sure to add all the salt and spices too.

Pour the combined mixture into the lined tray, quickly evening it out with a lightly oiled spoon if necessary. Top with a light sprinkling of flaked sea salt and set aside to cool.

Once set, break up the brittle with your hands or something heavy (a rolling pin will do the trick). Store covered in a cool, dry, place, and eat within a day or two.

Whisky Tablet —

I know a few purists who will curse me for deigning to put whisky in my tablet, but I rather like it. If you'd prefer a more traditional tablet experience, feel free to omit the whisky; either way this recipe will get you a melt-in-the-mouth sweet treat much like the kind that's been made for decades. It's a bit of a project (it takes a lot of standing and stirring), but in my opinion is well worth the effort.

Makes: 81 1-inch square pieces
Preparation time: 4 hours (2 hours active)

Ingredients -

125g vegan butter
(plus extra to grease the tin)
1kg golden caster sugar
400ml coconut milk
250ml coconut cream
1 tsp vanilla extract
60ml good-quality vegan whisky

Directions -

Grease a 9-inch square baking tin with vegan butter and set aside.

Place the sugar, coconut milk, and coconut cream into a large cooking pot. Place over a low heat and stir occasionally till the sugar has dissolved. Add in the butter and stir till melted.

Increase the heat to medium-high and allow the mixture to boil. Stir continuously with a wooden spoon until it reaches soft-ball stage (120 degrees Celsius or 248 Fahrenheit); if you know how to recognise this stage by sight, go for it, otherwise use a thermometer.

Add in the vanilla and the whisky (if using) and stir to combine.

Using an electric whisk, beat the mixture in the pot till it thickens up almost to setting point. When it's pretty thick, but still liquid, pour the mixture out into your greased tin and set aside to cool.

After 25 minutes, score the tablet into roughly 1-inch squares.

Leave to set for another 2-3 hours, cut, then serve or store in an airtight container in a cool, dry place.

Hazelnut and Amaretto Chocolate Truffles —

These things are little bites of joy. Wrapping them in gold foil and building them into a pyramid is completely optional.

Makes: 10 truffles
Preparation time: 8 hours 40 minutes (30 minutes active)

Ingredients -

250g good-quality vegan dark chocolate, chopped into small, even pieces
3 tbsp flavourless coconut oil
125ml non-sweet soy cream
1 vanilla pod, innards of
2 tbsp caster sugar
2 tbsp amaretto
80g chopped toasted hazelnuts
10 whole hazelnuts
A **pinch** of ground sea salt

Directions -

Place 150g of the chocolate along with the coconut oil into a bain-marie (or a heatproof bowl over a small saucepan with a little water in). Stirring occasionally, melt till smooth.

In a small or medium saucepan, heat the cream with the caster sugar till just hot. Remove from the heat and stir in the amaretto and vanilla.

Slowly pour the melted chocolate into the cream (not the other way around), stirring as you do. Leave to cool, then cover with cling film and refrigerate overnight.

Once the ganache is set, remove it from the fridge and tip out the chopped hazelnuts into a dish. Take out a tablespoon of the ganache, push a whole hazelnut into the middle, and roll into a ball with your hands. Do the same with all the ganache, then pop the balls in the freezer for 10 minutes. Meanwhile, melt the remaining chocolate in a bain-marie the same way as before. Remove the ganache balls from the freezer, then dip each one in the melted chocolate, then in the hazelnuts, making sure the ball is completely covered with both layers. Place the truffles on a plate and refrigerate till fully set.

Serve and enjoy! Store refrigerated in an airtight container for up to 4 days

Rose Turkish Delight —

There are some things that I feel just don't need changing, and rose Turkish delight is one of them.
Make like The Snow Queen and magic up your own endless supply of this gooey, sweet treat.

Makes: 81 1- inch square pieces
Preparation time: 2 hours

Ingredients -

Vegetable oil (to grease the tin)
800g caster sugar
2 tsp lemon juice
1l cold water
160g cornflour
(plus an extra **40g** for dusting)
1 tsp cream of tartar
1.5 tbsp rosewater
4-5 drops of red or pink food colouring
160g icing sugar

Directions -

Grease a 9-inch square baking tin with a little vegetable oil. Line with cling film then oil this too.

Add the sugar, lemon juice, and 375ml of the water to a large, heavy saucepan. Place over a medium heat and stir till the sugar dissolves and the mixture boils. Then reduce the heat and simmer gently, without stirring, until the mixture reaches soft-ball stage (120 degrees Celsius or 248 Fahrenheit). Your best bet is to measure this with a thermometer, although you can test the mixture by dropping a little into some cold water; if it pools at the bottom and can be removed and squashed into a ball, it's ready. Remove the pan from the heat and set aside.

In a large, heavy cooking pot stir together 160g of cornflour and the cream of tartar. Gradually mix in the remaining water until no lumps remain; I like to do this with an electric hand whisk. Keep whisking till the mixture boils and becomes a thick, gloopy paste.

Slowly pour the hot sugar syrup into the cornflour mixture, whisking constantly. Reduce the heat to low and simmer for 45-60 minutes, or till the mixture is thick and a quite deep golden-brown colour.

Stir in the rosewater and food colouring; when the colour is uniform, pour the mixture into the prepared tin. Shake the tin or use a lightly oiled spoon to even the mixture out. Put aside to cool and set overnight.

Sift the icing sugar and the extra cornflour onto a plate or board. Turn the Turkish delight out on top of this and cut into roughly 1-inch squares with a lightly oiled knife. Roll the pieces in the sugar mixture till very well coated.

The fresher the Turkish delight is when you eat it, the better it will be. If necessary, store it in an airtight container with sheets of greaseproof paper and plenty of the sugar mixture between each layer.

All text and photographs © Emily Wilkinson, 2015. www.morelfood.com

All rights reserved. No part of this publication may be reproduced or transmitted in any form or by any means, electronic or mechanical, including photocopying, recording, or any information storage or retrieval system, without prior permission in writing from the author, Emily Wilkinson.

¯_(ツ)_/¯